SANTIAGO CALATRAVA

Structures in Movement

santiago CALATRAVA

Structures in Movement

The Architecture of Santiago Calatrava

An Exhibition Conceived and Curated by

Alexander Tzonis

MEADOWS MUSEUM

Southern Methodist University
Dallas, Texas
2001

Meadows Museum
Southern Methodist University
Dallas, Texas 75275

ISBN 0-935-937-15-3 (Hardcover edition)
ISBN 0-935-937-16-3 (Softcover edition)

First edition, 2001.

© 2001 by Meadows Museum.

Front Cover:
Oriente Station, Lisbon, Portugal, 1993-98
Sculpture, 2000

Back Cover:
Alamillo Bridge & Cartuja Viaduct, Seville, Spain, 1987-92
Sculpture, 2000

Frontispiece pages 2 &3:
Calatrava's human figures, watercolor

Designed and produced by James A. Ledbetter, Dallas

Printed in Hong Kong by South China Printing Company (1988) Ltd.

CONTENTS

COMMUNITIES
FOUNDATION
OF TEXAS

Creating a Lasting Legacy for Today's Philanthropists

What a proud and exciting time for Southern Methodist University, the Meadows Museum, and all of Dallas!

Communities Foundation of Texas is delighted to share in the well-deserved pride generated by this grand inaugural exhibit. It is, indeed, a privilege to partner with educators, fellow philanthropists, arts advocates and our civic leaders to showcase the extraordinary work of Spanish architect, artist and engineer Santiago Calatrava in this magnificent new facility.

The Foundation's investment in this project, on behalf of the Margot W. and Ben H. Mitchell Fund, reflects Communities Foundation of Texas' deep commitment to the arts and education and to fulfilling the generous legacy of our donors. Spanning 50 years, our contributions also represent confidence in the future—in the vision and structure of things to come. As Calatrava's work explores innovative ways to bridge space, we function in this community to creatively enhance important links between students and artists, donors, and projects, cities and a higher quality of life for all citizens.

Communities Foundation of Texas joins in welcoming Santiago Calatrava, the 15th recipient of the Algur H. Meadows Awards for Excellence in the Arts. And we thank SMU's Meadows School of the Arts for introducing Calatrava's work to Texas and using the occasion of the opening of this new museum to enhance the visibility and stature of the City of Dallas in the international arts arena.

Charles J. Wyly, Jr.   Edward M. Fjordbak
Chairman   President

Acknowledgements

The creative efforts of many people are necessary for the realization of projects such as this book and the related exhibition at Meadows Museum in Dallas, *Poetics of Movement: The Architecture of Santiago Calatrava* (March 25 – August 5, 2001) . The subject of both, Santiago Calatrava, has our profound gratitude both for creating this extraordinary body of work and for his interest in the exhibition itself. All of us involved also thank both Robertina Calatrava and Kim Marangoni for their support and many forms of assistance at the Zürich end of these efforts. The exhibition was conceived and curated by Professor Alexander Tzonis, University of Technology Delft, and designed by Alkistis Rodi and Alexander Tzonis, Athens Design Knowledge Studio. To them we owe immeasurable gratitude.

In Dallas, the support of both the staff of Meadows Museum and of key people in the Meadows School of the Arts was essential. Both Dr. Carole Brandt, dean of the Meadows School of the Arts, and associate dean P. Gregory Warden provided ongoing encouragement, energy, and effort at all stages of the planning and realization of the exhibition. The ongoing interest of The Meadows Foundation continues to reassure us in all that we do. The complex logistics of bringing both the exhibition and this publication to completion were handled with grace and effectiveness by Meadows Museum staff members Jack Powers, Barbara Pierce, and Nathan Augustine. Further greatly appreciated assistance came from Kris Westerson and Maia Toteva. A special debt of gratitude is owed James A. Ledbetter, who did far more than the beautiful design of this publication by helping at a basic organizational and editorial level as well.

Underwriting for both this publication and the exhibition was provided by Communities Foundation of Texas through the Margot W. and Ben H. Mitchell Fund. Our profound thanks goes to the Foundation and to its officers, chairman Charles J. Wyly, Jr. and president Edward M. Fjordbak.

Director's Preface

This publication accompanies the inaugural special exhibition in a magnificent new building for the Meadows Museum, which opened on the campus of Southern Methodist University in late March of 2001. Santiago Calatrava was chosen as the subject of this exhibition because he is among Spain's greatest living practitioners in the visual arts, and Meadows Museum's permanent collection is devoted exclusively to the arts of Spain and the Hispanic world.

We were fortunate that Dr. Calatrava's choice for the curator of the exhibition, Professor Alexander Tzonis of the University of Technology Delft, graciously agreed to conceive and curate the exhibition entitled *Poetics of Movement: The Architecture of Santiago Calatrava*. In addition to contributing the introductory essay for this publication, Professor Tzonis worked with Dr. Calatrava in the selection of the project models, drawings, and sculptures which comprise the Dallas exhibition. He also designed the exhibition in conjunction with Alkistis Rodi at Athens Design Knowledge Studio.

The centrality of visual art – especially sculpture and drawing, the latter often in painterly washes – in the creative process of Santiago Calatrava makes the presentation of his work in an art museum particularly appropriate. Among themes of creative thought and process to which Calatrava returns in conversation is the role of the architect as artist and of architecture as art. The seamless union he envisions for the two is embodied in his own practice and work. Given Calatrava's depth of training in engineering, his insistence on the aesthetic swing of the pendulum as well sets him apart and reveals why even such primarily functional structures as bridges become under Calatrava's touch objects of sensuous beauty.

There is a centuries old Spanish and greater Mediterranean design tradition in which structural utility and organic beauty of form unite. Growing from this tradition is the work of Calatrava's fellow Catalan, Antoni Gaudí, with its daringly off-balance appearing slanted columns and geometrically varied arches. In the mid-twentieth century, two engineer-architects took concrete structural members and made them into architectural art, the Italian Pier Luigi Nervi and Félix Candela. Candela, whom Calatrava knew, was Spanish born, but emigrated to Mexico in 1939, where he built thin-shelled concrete structures whose design grew from hyperbolic parabolas. In his own wedding of structural necessity with forms which seem to have grown naturally and at times almost to take flight, Santiago Calatrava is the heir and continuer of this Mediterranean mode and is today bringing it to our country in his various North American commissions.

John Lunsford
Director
Meadows Museum

Santiago Calatrava

Structures in Movement

An Exhibition Conceived and Curated by Professor Alexander Tzonis,
University of Technology Delft

INTRODUCTION

Structure and movement seem to be antithetical, not to say mutually exclusive. Intuitively, most people assume that structures are rigid and stable, not mobile. Even Leonardo da Vinci believed that "the first and most important thing (in a structure) is stability (*permanentia*)." Elastic, shaky, loose structures induce visions of buckling, cracking, snapping, toppling over. They trigger a feeling of fear. They raise doubt and perhaps a sense of danger. They may even suggest how temporary artifacts are and metaphorically allude to the transience or even arbitrariness of mental and institutional constructs. No wonder designers of structures have traditionally tried to express, emphasize, and celebrate stability, or *stasis*.

But for structures, of course, movement is a basic fact of life. They are never at rest. The more we know about their behavior, the more we realize how, although apparently immobile, they undiscernibly although perpetually move. They slide and shudder, bend and bow, sway and tremble. Movement is everywhere in buildings. They not only move themselves, inescapably they constitute receptacles and channels for the movement of people and things. Moreover, structures are put together through movement and it is through movement that they are taken apart.

Today, the awareness of movement in our own lives is stronger than ever before. Speed, mobility, and change dominate our life. Perhaps this is why in the work of architects in general movement has increasingly replaced *stasis* as the main structural, symbolic, and functional preoccupation. What distinguishes Santiago Calatrava from other architects is that he expresses this more profoundly, intensely, and *universally* than anyone else.

Santiago Calatrava

There are very few designers of our time who can be called universal. Santiago Calatrava is one of these. In his numerous buildings, engineering projects, drawings, sculpture, and furniture design, he has developed a unique poetics of morphology meshing structure and movement, overcoming the abyss that separates art from science and technology, a *poetics of movement.*

Although the idea of movement in architecture has not been a central concept, there has been a long line of important writers, architects, and engineers who have longed for structures to be able to break free of the straightjacket of rigid firmness and have thought of ways of bringing movement into structures. I will try to situate the work of Calatrava, his poetics of movement, and his patient research,[1] within this context.

One of the earliest literary references to a moving structure is to be found in Exodus, chapter 33, where a "pillar of cloud" swirls down from the sky and stands at the tabernacle door in front of Moses. The subsequent spiral form of the column that comes to be called the Solomonic Order in mannerist architecture originates in that passage. Moving structures also appear in a literary genre made up of tales containing descriptions of marvelous projects and referred to as *Mirabilia,* dating from the tenth century and then becoming prominent in Europe from the twelfth to the end of the fourteenth century. In the sixteenth century, the representation of movement in buildings becomes a concern of practicing architects. According to Heinrich Wölfflin, Michelangelo's Palazzo dei Conservatori expresses "an unceasing, restless struggle for liberty" and a "wild desire for movement."[2] Movement continues to play a significant role in seventeenth and eighteenth century architecture, which incorporates within the landscape "mobiles," "water structures," and pyrotechnics. Clearly, the work of Santiago Calatrava belongs to this tradition, which has moved from the periphery to the heart of design today. Nevertheless, what makes his work so different from any other is the strength of commitment, the ingenuity, and the diversity of ways through which his structures incorporate movement.

From his early years as a student at the Art Academy in Valencia, in the mid-1960s, Calatrava obsessively drew human bodies in movement, often using the so-called "Goya five point exercise" to generate unexpected figures in movement, a practice he still follows. A decade later, at the Federal Polytechnic University of Zürich, movement was the subject of his Ph.D. dissertation, *The Foldability of Space Frames.*[3] Its objective was to develop a method for transforming three-dimensional space frames into planar shapes and lines by moving their elements. The two types of work are very different. The one is pictorial and analogical, the other quantitative and analytical; the first carried out in an "Apollonian" spirit, the second in a "Dionysian" one.[4] However, in the framework of his design-universalism, Calatrava engaged both as complementary tools of inquiry toward the same end, the development of a poetics of movement. He still employs both tools during the creative process. Repeatedly, the form of a scheme emerges by analogy to a dancer's gesture or the shape of the moving body of a bird or a bull. At the same time, many of the schemes and mechanisms of folding building elements—doors, canopies, and roofs—are based on the theoretical material of the dissertation. In a less obvious way the enigmatic configurations of the series of sculptures of the **Aegean Circle** also emerge out of the knowledge developed in the dissertation. The folding frames of the space structures he studied are not only useful for conceiving the form of possible mobile containers. The legs of the frames, hinged at one point, as they fold trace circles or other more complex curves, cycloids, epicycloids, cardioids, parabolas, or hyperbolas. They can be used, therefore, as mechanical devices called *linkages*,[5] a kind of complex "compass" for generating new shapes and more intricate surfaces such as are found in many of Calatrava's sculptures, and especially in the series the Aegean Circle.

As we mentioned above, the most obvious way structures relate to movement is as vessels containing circulation of people or objects. This, by definition, is the case of infrastructure projects, bridges, stations, as well as buildings involving moving masses. **The Stadelhofen Station**, a 270 meter-long train station in Zürich, was Calatrava's earliest major work. It was immediately proclaimed a most successful integration of public transportation in an urban context and a natural setting. But it was also the outcome of Calatrava's capability to conceive it as a well-formed organism made of different interacting flows rather than as a composition of static spaces. Within the complex, the fast regular flow of trains along the tracks cutting through the ground level integrates with the hasty crowds entering and leaving the vehicles, approaching and leaving the station, ascending, descending, walking through the shopping mall, under the tracks and over three steel bridges.

As noted, incorporating mobile parts in a project is another direct way of bringing movement into a structure, as in the dome for the **Reichstag Conversion** Competition, that was meant to open and close like a gigantic flower. The same with the roof of the **Planetarium** of the **Science Center** in **Valencia**, intended to shut and retract like the lids of a colossal, cyclopic eye gazing into the sky. In an earlier work, one of Calatrava's first projects, the **Ernstings Warehouse and Distribution Center** in **Coesfeld, Westfalen**, he designed a swaying garage door combining functional requirements with the poetics of movement. When the door is lifted, it appears to emulate the slow movement of a bending knee cladding folding as if it is "cloth." The image of cloth is present on the cladding of the "curtain wall" that surrounds the building, taking a shape as if fluttering in the breeze. By felicitous coincidence, Ernstings is a textile firm, which makes the blowing curtain effect even happier. The contrast between the metallic material of the elements and their waving geometry surrounds the building with an unreal, dream-like atmosphere.

This is the case also with the kinetic, wing-like sculptures, both constructed in concrete, by Calatrava: the **Concrete Pavilion** for **Swissbau** of 1989 in Basle called "Shadow Machine" and the similar piece that Calatrava exhibited at the Museum of Modern Art in New York in 1993.

Increasingly, as the complexity of Calatrava's projects grows and the sophistication of their technology advances, the work manifests a tendency to produce the wildest metaphors. As Liane Lefaivre observes,[6] borrowing a concept of Freud, Calatrava invites us to "dream-work" in an almost Buñuel-like way, to experience structures breaking free from the static world entering another kind of movement, that of generating possible worlds, of fulfilling a wish, of acting out a desire. Thus, concrete, categorized in the minds of most people as a hard and heavy material, is cast in the shape of the body of a dolphin and suddenly appears to strangely carry out the graceful movement of the hands of a dancer or the movement of the wings of a bird. Calatrava appears here using movement as the heir of the surrealist artists, movie directors, and poets that Lewis Mumford once welcomed in New York as a necessary component of our machine civilization.[7]

What we observe above is that a less explicit way for bringing movement into a structure is by turning its elements into icons, thus giving them an explicit meaning related to movement, an approach known in the nineteenth century as *architecture parlante*. Several architects, and more recently Eero Saarinen, followed this approach. Calatrava gave a shape to the roof structure for the **IBA Squash Complex** for Berlin that resembles a gigantic insect. Similarly, a few years later, the **Lyon Airport Station**, Satolas, and the **Tenerife Opera House** are configured imitating the silhouettes of flying birds. Such schemes work mentally by triggering associative memory, a very basic cognitive faculty, rather than reflection. Their impact is immediate and it leads to widely appreciated popular projects.

Calatrava's structures also appear to imitate vegetable forms. The most conspicuous is the **Oriente Station** in Lisbon. There is a long tradition of attaching such elements to structural members of buildings, as in the case of the acanthus on the Greek and Roman Corinthian capitals. Similarly, vegetal forms were imitated in the columnar members of the famous Valencia building Lonja del Mercado, a building that much impressed Calatrava as a child. They are also seen in the seventeenth and eighteenth century designs by José and Joaquín de Churriguera and, more recently, in the "organic" configurations of Louis Sullivan, Hector Guimard, and Victor Horta. Plant-like structures in these cases are more than decorative depictions. They suggest a gradual pace of growth and thus imply that structures like plants are not, or do not have to be, static. To remember D'Arcy Thompson, the form of a structure is a result of movement. It is a response to different load conditions that yields a well-formed structure whose "superfluous material has been removed" gradually, as if through evolution.[8]

If this idea is taken one step further, the preservation of the memory of the genesis of the form of structures implies movement. Like the tissue of natural objects, the stuff of artificial structures is the result of specific acts that involve movement: carrying, raising, pouring, welding, bonding, assembling, nailing, joining, fastening. It was Ruskin, pre-empting D'Arcy Thompson, who first wrote about "growth and form" in his *Modern Painters*, linking it with memory. For Ruskin, structures that bear the mark of the forces that generated them preserve the memory of their creation and have a special value both as knowledge and as moral stance in relation to human community. Thus, as opposed to erasing the traces of the genesis and evolution of an object, Ruskin[9] recommended their preservation.

A century later, Paul Valéry[10] stated epigrammatically: "the work does not have to erase the traces of the work." He was interested in creative process and in documenting it. More specifically, he was referring to the importance of the sketches of artists like Degas as means to understand their finished major works. Valéry's words suggest a broader idea about the work of art. A subtle way to keep this memory, beyond associative mimetic memory mechanisms and with profound philosophical, cognitive, and moral significance, is by giving to the structure a configuration that evokes a reflective stance from the viewer toward the artifact. This approach characterizes Calatrava's work.

The roots of the approach go back to antiquity, to the search to develop a conceptual frame for representing the body in motion in sculpture. The ancient sculptor and writer Polyclitos is credited with establishing the fundamentals of a theory, in his book *The Canon*, written in the fifth century B.C. But it was Quintilian, the Roman theoretician of rhetoric and aesthetics, who introduced the term *contraposto*, to name it.[11] The literal meaning of the term is "counter position." We do not know the exact content of the essay by Polyclitos, which has been lost, but later authors tell us that he prescribed the position of the parts of the human body. The body should be resting on one leg, pushed a little to the rear, with the other leg bent at the knee and applying less pressure. The chest, while tilted backward, should be slightly bent, and the head should lean to the side in the opposite direction to the chest. This "counter posing" of the members of the body was seen as expressing graceful movement, Polyclitos himself practicing it in his own work.

Clearly, Polyclitos did not provide instructions for depicting the image of specific, real-life moving bodies. As indicated by the very concept of *The Canon*, he created an abstract system of rules based on axes and a set of relationships among them. This abstract knowledge was drawn from the body image but does not have to be observational. It was a powerful framework, able to capture the most significant characteristics of any kind of body in motion with the potential to be applicable to any kind of structure.

We see the theory revived and revised by Giovanni Paolo Lomazzo (1584).[12] Lomazzo proposed the *figura serpentinata*, or S-form as he called it, because it resembled that letter. Lomazzo credited Michelangelo, who was planning to write on the idea of movement, with originating the idea of the "serpent-like figure." Lomazzo's S-form was a more abstract and reductive schema than *contraposto*, which he related to "the flame of fire." *Contraposto* dominated Western Art centuries after its interpretation by Lomazzo and emerges unexpectedly in the formal structure of works as different as Francisco de Goya's *La vendimia o el otoño* or Marcel Duchamp's *Nude Descending a Staircase*.

What is interesting in contraposto and the serpentine figure is that, although they primarily represent the moving body, they are abstract spatial concepts, deeply rooted cognitive schemata that can be projected to any other object. They capture the moment when a structure, as if arrested by an invisible power, is poised in a state of equilibrium and immobility, on the brink of imminent collapse. One can easily recognize both *contraposto* and the *figura serpentinata* in almost all the works of Calatrava as a signature figure: the pergola supports at Stadelhofen Station, leaning to reach out, only to return, the **Montjuïc Communications Tower**, and in the supports of the remodeling for the **Church of St. John the Divine** in New York.

The eighteenth century philosopher, Gotthold Ephraim Lessing, in his epoch-making book comparing art and poetry entitled *Laocoon*,[13] went further in developing a theory explaining how immobile figures, in general, might imply movement. The example he used was the newly discovered, much discussed sculpture in his time, picturing Laocoon and his sons struggling as they are devoured by snakes, a seething mass of entwining serpentine lines and volumes.

Lessing's idea was that the artist, as opposed to the writer, "can use but a single moment of action . . . this single moment he makes as pregnant as possible." The metaphor of pregnant indicated a *non finito* process of generation—to use a category attributed to Michelangelo's sculptures in a state of partial benign incompleteness, the body or the face of a person barely emerging from the mass of the unworked material. It suggested the capability of a given figure in its present immobile state to recall a past and suggest a future state. In this single suspended moment, Lessing writes, the "artist unites two distinct points of time, what has occurred before and what is to follow."

And thus we sense the pregnant moment in the single arch of the **La Devesa Bridge** in Ripoll, swerving on the point of collapse, soaring on its ascent, or in the mast of the **Alamillo Bridge** in Seville, its forty-meter-long pylon now "as if" falling, now "as though" rising.

Calatrava appears to join the aesthetic concept of the pregnant moment with the engineering notion of the "critical point"—that is, the point beyond which, if a certain variable in design is exceeded, the interatomic bonds of the material of the structure break and collapse. He appears to concentrate loads to a critical point, slimming sections to a critical extent, raising the slope lines to a critical degree, and enjoying the results like an acrobat or even more like a shrewd dancer performing a physical feat. There is a deeper reward, however, here. We are led to envision in the form of the structure, as D'Arcy Thompson[14] always invited us to do, the diagram of operating forces. The diagram is vivid because of the articulated extremes of the seemingly contradictory form of the structure. Far from sublime, from arousing feelings of irrational fear, the effect of these critical conditions is cognitive. It allows two contrary readings simultaneously, like a Rubin diagram. The structure falls, then doesn't.

Calatrava's structures might seem at this point contradictory, appearing to aim at two opposed goals. The contradiction, however, is only a surface one. The paradoxes his structures violate are common sense beliefs, naïve intuition, and banal expectations. They invite further thinking, broadening, deepening, and enriching of our understanding of the world. They stimulate reflection through oxymoron and paradox, ultimately leading to the search for an answer.

In the beginning of this essay we put forth the idea of a poetics of morphology engaging structure and movement, the *poetics of movement*, as central to Calatrava's creative process. It is an approach that offers a cultural vision of synthesis bringing together art, science, and technology. The exhibition demonstrates this idea and makes a pragmatic point. A necessary condition to improve our cities and landscapes today is to overcome the strictures among architecture, infrastructure, and sculpture, all three offering at the same time answers to problems but also invitations to new questions, epistemological and moral, and about the meaning of human action.

Beyond the obsession with form, problem-solving, critical inquiry, and dream working, Calatrava's work manifests a philosophical inquiry seeking to define a moral system for human action and desire through geometric reasoning. Calatrava's poetics of movement are instruments that solve posed problems as well as avenues opening new inquires for a vision of a better life. In this capacity they bring a message of hope and humanness.

NOTES

1   For further reading on the subject see: Alexander Tzonis and Liane Lefaivre, *Movement, Structure and the Work of Santiago Calatrava* (Basel: Birkhäuser, 1995). Alexander Tzonis, *Santiago Calatrava, The Poetics of Movement* (New York: Universe, 1999).

2   Heinrich Wölfflin, *Renaissance and Baroque* (London: Fontana Library, 1964; first published in German 1888). See in particular the chapter devoted to movement, 58-70.

3   Santiago Calatrava Valls, *Zur Faltbarkeit von Fachwerken* (Ph.D. Diss., Swiss Federal Institute of Technology, Zürich, 1981).

4   Alexander Tzonis and Liane Lefaivre, *Santiago Calatrava's Creative Process. Volume I: The Dissertation* and *Volume II: Sketchbooks* (Basel: Birkhäuser, 2000).

5   Richard Courant and Herbert Robbins, *What is Mathematics?* (New York, 1941) 155.

6   Private discussion with author.

7   Lewis Mumford, "Surrealism and Civilization," *The New Yorker* (Dec. 19, 1936).

8   D'Arcy Wentworth Thompson, *On Growth and Form, The Complete Revised Edition* (New York: Dover, 1992; first published 1942).

9   John Ruskin, *Modern Painters* (Oxford, 1843-1860). Volume 4.

10   Paul Valéry, *Degas, Danse, Dessin* (Paris: Gallimard, 1938).

11   Quintilian, *Institutio Oratoria*, trans. H.E. Butler (Cambridge: Loeb Library, 1980).

12   Giovanni Paolo Lomazzo, *Trattato dell'arte della pittura* (1584).

13   Gotthold Ephraim Lessing, *Laocoon, an Essay upon the Limits of Painting and Poetry* (New York: Noonday, 1957; first published as *Laokoon: oder Uber die Grenzen der Malerei und Poezie, 1766).*

14   D'Arcy Wentworth Thompson, *On Growth and Form, The Complete Revised Edition* (New York, Dover, 1992; first published 1942).

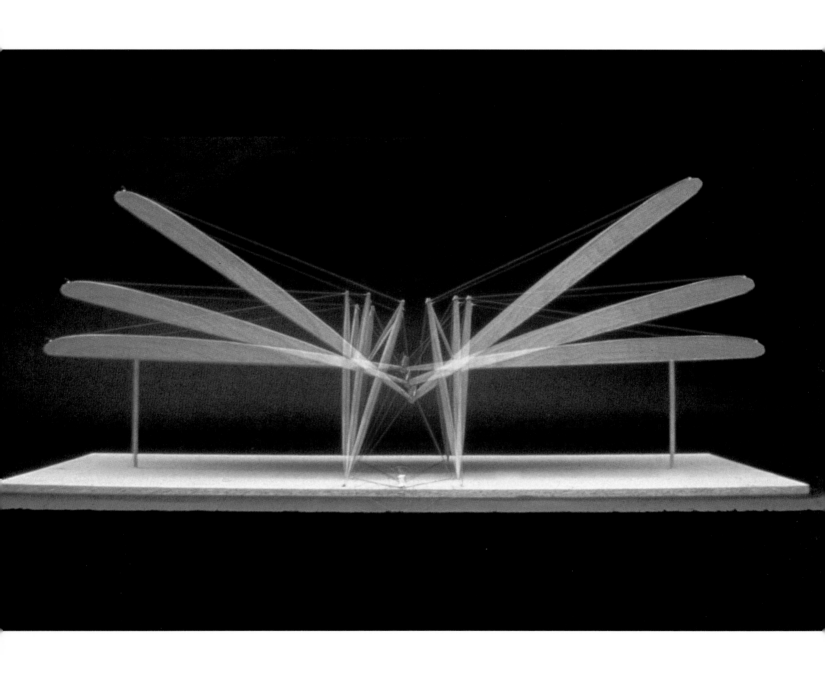

Genomy Projects

CHAPTER 1

Santiago Calatrava's diverse and rich oeuvre emerges out of a limited number of basic design strategies that can be traced back to a small number of early projects. They are seminal "genomy" schemes, the genetic pool from which most of the design ideas of his later work originate. Common to all these projects are basic major design strategies and design themes. These are born out of intensive design research employing a combination, unique for our time, of scientific analysis involving mathematical inquiries and dreamwork analogy embracing anthropomorphic and other biomorphic explorations. They optimize resources and performances, both *differentiating* elements of a structure and *profiling* individual elements. They give birth to "signature" morphological themes that establish the recognizable "Calatrava Style," an aesthetically rich "formal style" as well as an engineering "solution style:" the fluid, varying curved profiles; the palindrome silhouettes; the dialectic articulations of structure. Movement pulses throughout this structural morphology, explicitly expressed in the configuration of the structure but also tacitly implied in the shape of its fabric.

IBA Squash Complex
Berlin, Germany
1979

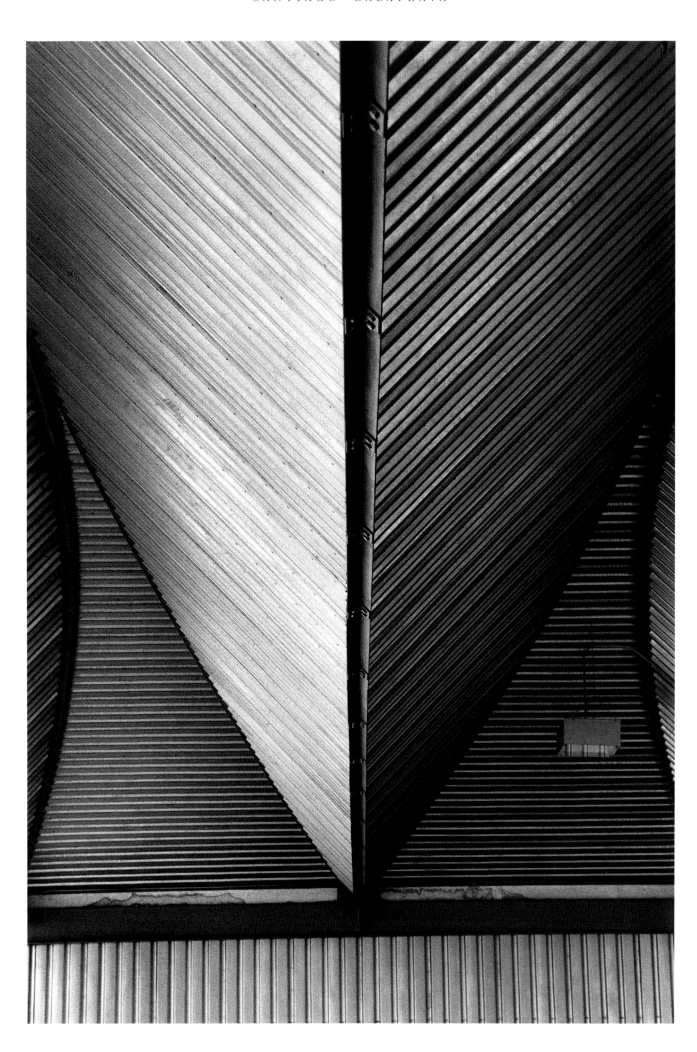

27

Above and facing page

Jakem Warehouse
Münchwilen, Switzerland
1983-84

28

Above and facing page

Ernstings Warehouse
Coesfeld, Germany
1983-85

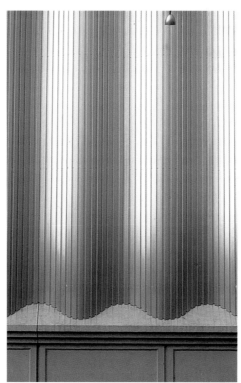

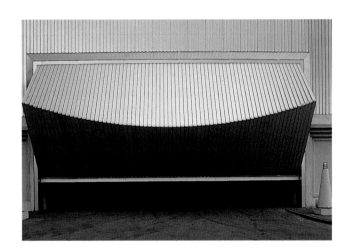

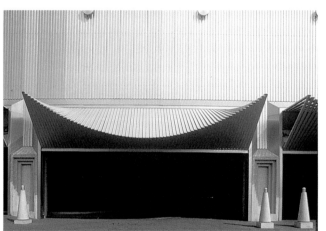

Above and facing page

Ernstings Warehouse
Coesfeld, Germany
1983-85

Above and facing page

Stadelhofen Station
Zürich, Switzerland
1983-90

32

33

Translation of the above inscription

the expression of the hands
the curves of the transition between elements
the gesture

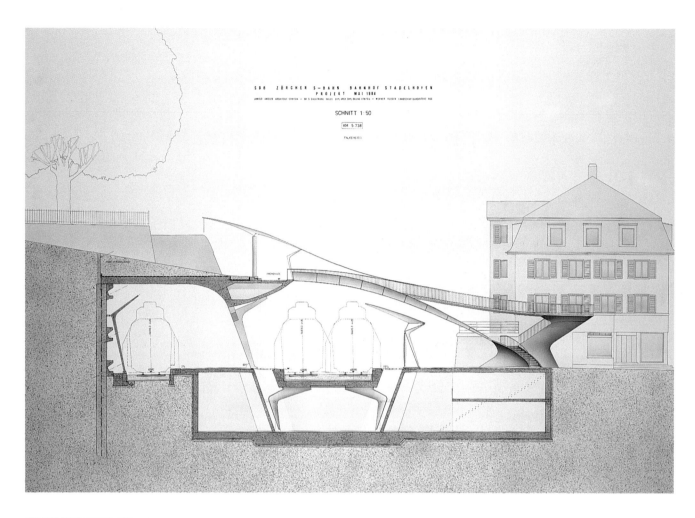

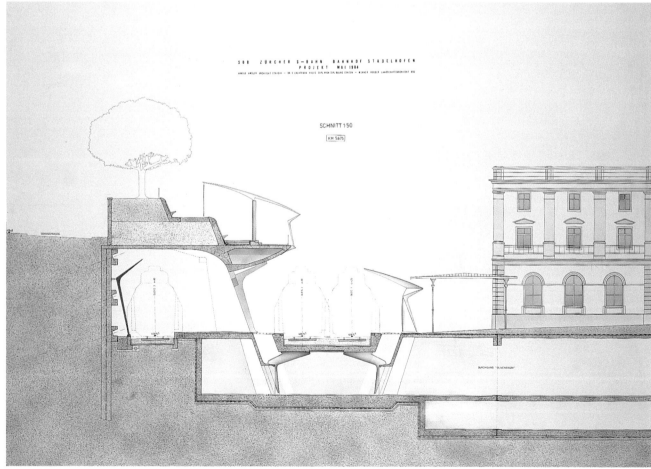

34

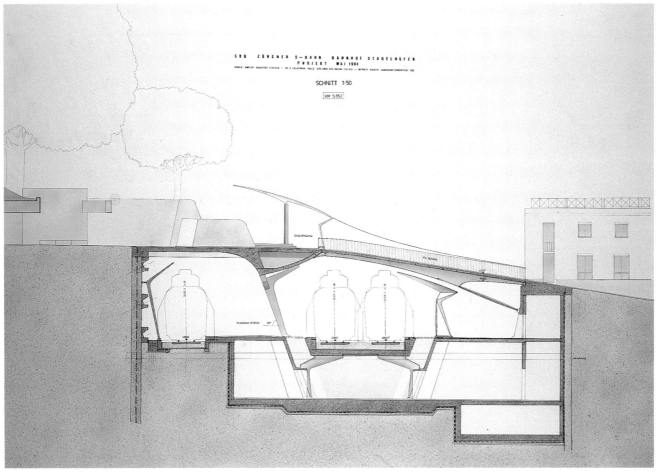

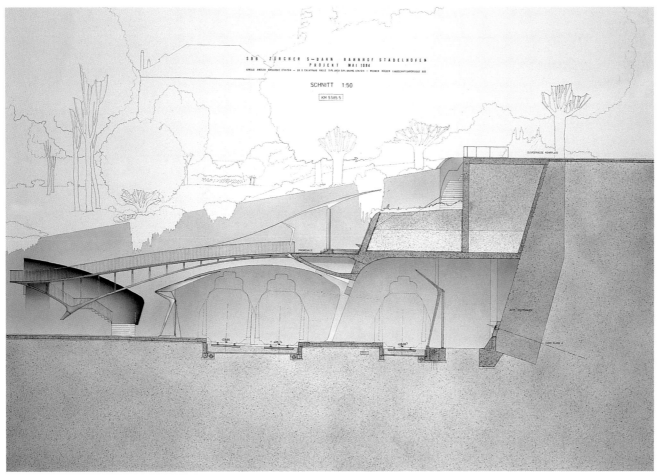

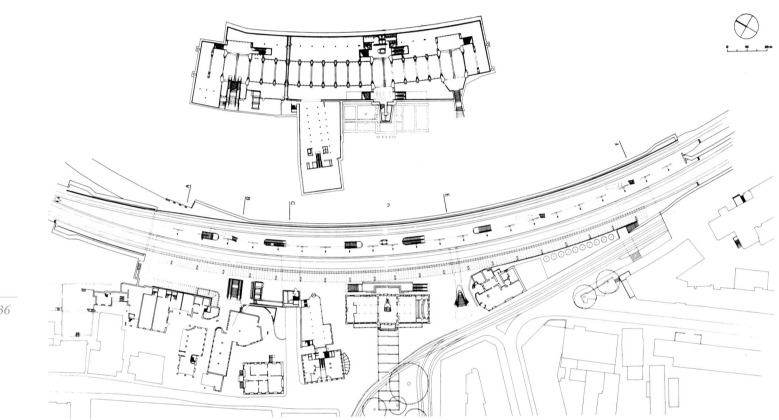

Pages 34, 35 and above

Stadelhofen Station
Zürich, Switzerland
1983-90

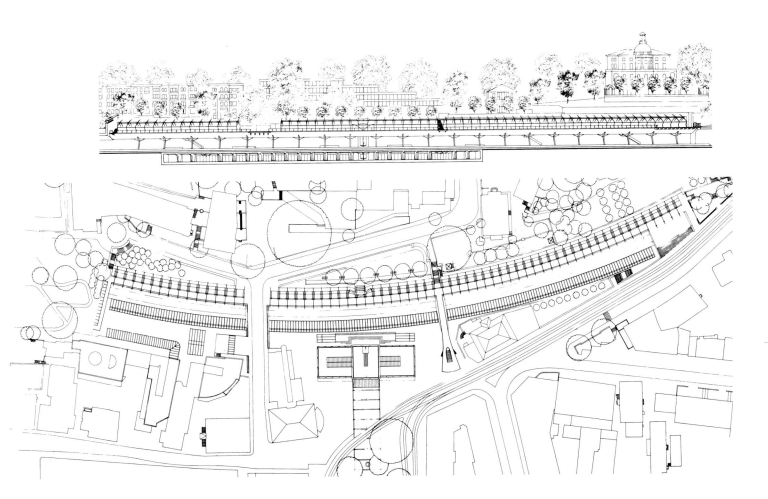

Stadelhofen Station
Zürich, Switzerland
1983-90

38

Wohlen High School, Roofs and Hall
Wohlen, Switzerland
1983-88

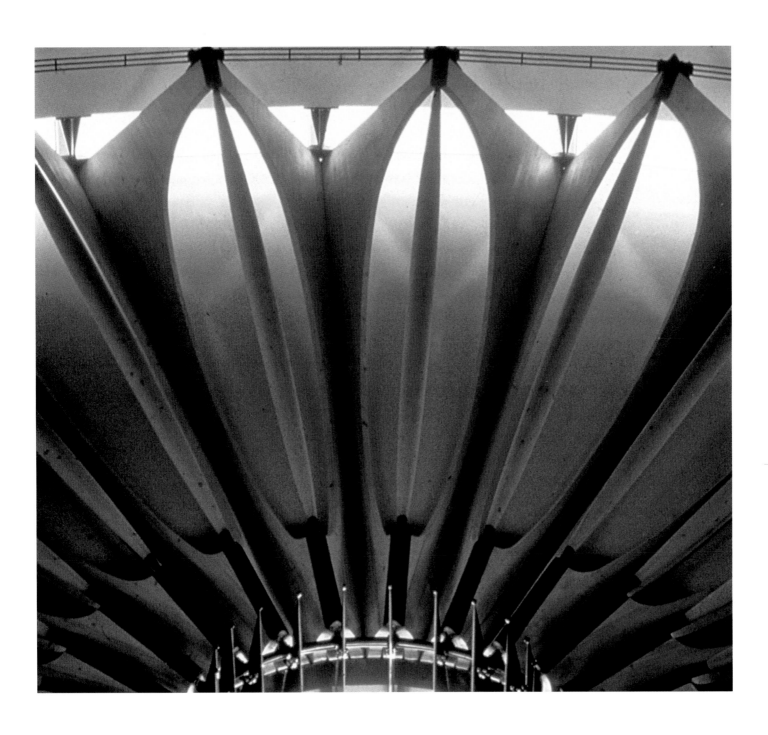

39

Wohlen High School, Roofs and Hall
Wohlen, Switzerland
1983-88

Wohlen High School, Roofs and Hall
Wohlen, Switzerland
1983-88

Wohlen High School, Roofs and Hall
Wohlen, Switzerland
1983-88

42

Wohlen High School, Roofs and Hall
Wohlen, Switzerland
1983-88

Wohlen High School, Roofs and Hall

Wohlen, Switzerland

1983-88

44

Bärenmatte Community Center
Suhr, Switzerland
1984-88

Bärenmatte Community Center
Suhr, Switzerland
1984-88

46

Bärenmatte Community Center
Suhr, Switzerland
1984-88

Bärenmatte Community Center
Suhr, Switzerland
1984-88

48

Bach de Roda - Felipe II Bridge
Barcelona, Spain
1984-87

Bach de Roda - Felipe II Bridge
Barcelona, Spain
1984-87

51

Above and facing page

Tabourettli Theatre
Basle, Switzerland
1986-87

Above and facing page

BCE Place: Galleria & Heritage Square
Toronto, Canada
1987-92

Above and facing page

BCE Place: Galleria & Heritage Square
Toronto, Canada
1987-92

56

BCE Place: Galleria & Heritage Square
Toronto, Canada
1987-92

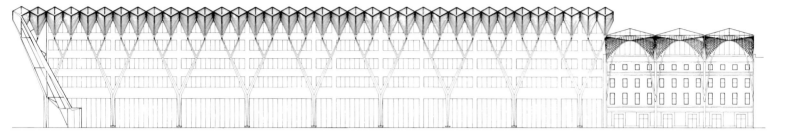

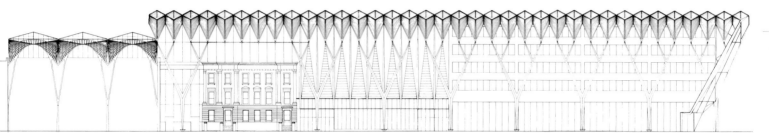

LONGITUDINAL SECTIONS
1:200

BCE Place: Galleria & Heritage Square
Toronto, Canada
1987-92

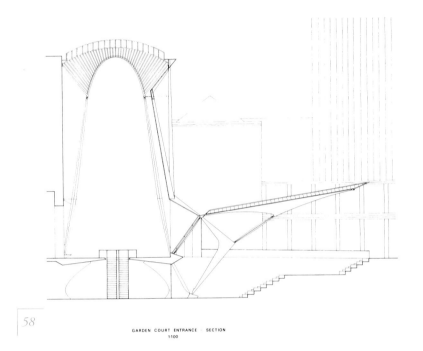

GARDEN COURT ENTRANCE · SECTION
1100

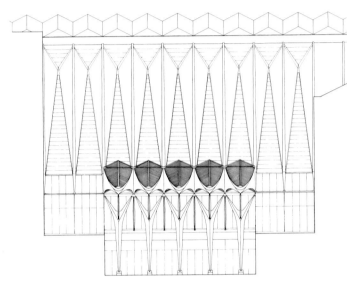

GARDEN COURT ENTRANCE · ELEVATION
1100

58

BCE Place: Galleria & Heritage Square
Toronto, Canada
1987-92

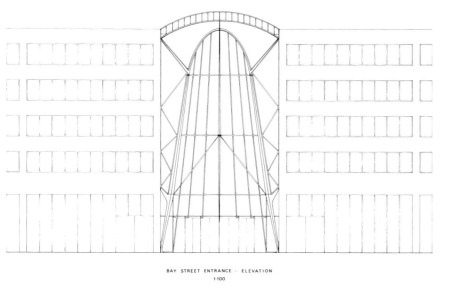

BAY STREET ENTRANCE : ELEVATION
1:100

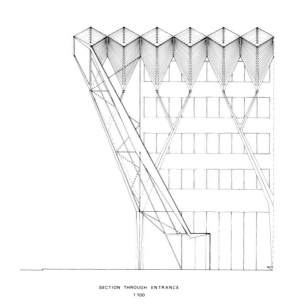

SECTION THROUGH ENTRANCE
1:100

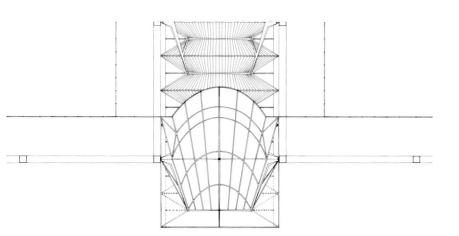

VIEW OF ENTRANCE CANOPY
1:100

BCE Place: Galleria & Heritage Square
Toronto, Canada
1987-92

Oudry-Mesly Footbridge
Créteil-Paris, France
1987-88

Oudry-Mesly Footbridge
Créteil-Paris, France
1987-88

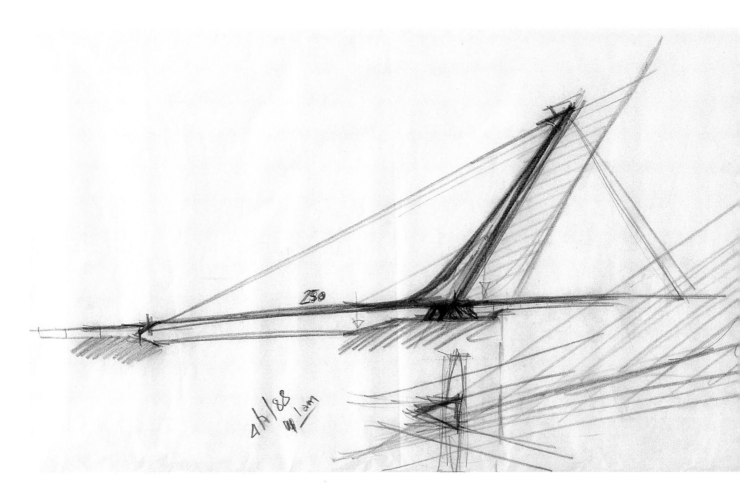

Above and facing page

Alamillo Bridge & Cartuja Viaduct
Seville, Spain
1987-92

Commitment
to Site

CHAPTER 2

Soon after Calatrava finished the first exploratory projects he became
involved in a number of new, ambitious, large-scale, and more complex
projects. Characteristic of this work is the recruitment and recombina-
tion of design inventions conceived in the early, germinal years of his
career. Formal motifs, spatial themes, and design stories involving
structure and movement familiar from earlier work are reinterpreted.
As Calatrava becomes increasingly preoccupied with the uniqueness
and character of each given site these precedents are rethought and
reinvented. Such an engagement with existing conditions and the
constraints of the surrounding environment embraces both the hidden
adversities and the latent potentials of the site. Many projects are
located in harsh urban environments—peripheral, abandoned, and
hopeless areas—, others in historically and aesthetically rich
landscapes. Calatrava faces the challenge of both situations and
embraces both realities with equal commitment and passion.

65

Montjuïc Communications Tower
Barcelona, Spain
1989-92

66

Lusitania Bridge
Mérida, Spain
1988-91

Lusitania Bridge
Mérida, Spain
1988-91

68

Montjuïc Communications Tower
Barcelona, Spain
1989-92

Montjuïc Communications Tower
Barcelona, Spain
1989-92

Lyon Airport Station
Satolas-Lyon, France
1989-94

Lyon Airport Station
Satolas-Lyon, France
1989-94

72

Puerto Bridge
Ondarroa, Spain
1989-95

Puerto Bridge
Ondarroa, Spain
1989-95

74

La Devesa Footbridge
Ripoll, Spain
1989-91

La Devesa Footbridge
Ripoll, Spain
1989-91

Campo Volantin Footbridge
Bilbao, Spain
1990-97

Campo Volantin Footbridge

Bilbao, Spain

1990-97

Above and facing page

Campo Volantin Footbridge
Bilbao, Spain
1990-97

Sondica Airport
Bilbao, Spain
1990-

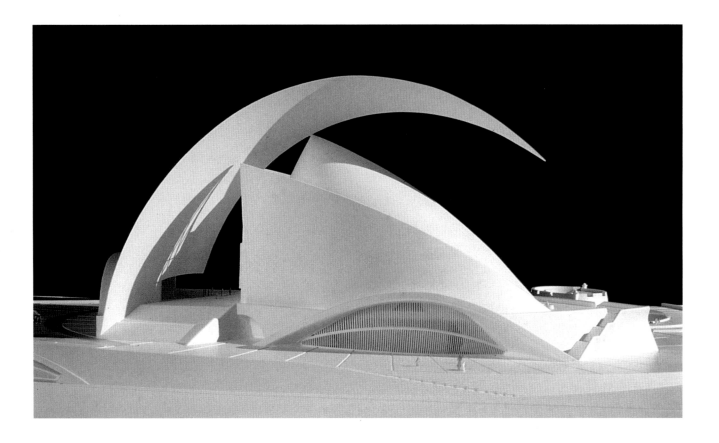

Tenerife Opera House
Tenerife, Spain
1991-

Kuwait Pavillion
Seville, Spain
1991-92

Kuwait Pavillion
Seville, Spain
1991-92

84

Ciudad de las Artes y de las Ciencias
Valencia, Spain
1991-2000

Ciudad de las Artes y de las Ciencias
Valencia, Spain
1991-2000

Above and facing page

Ciudad de las Artes y de las Ciencias
Valencia, Spain
1991-2000

88

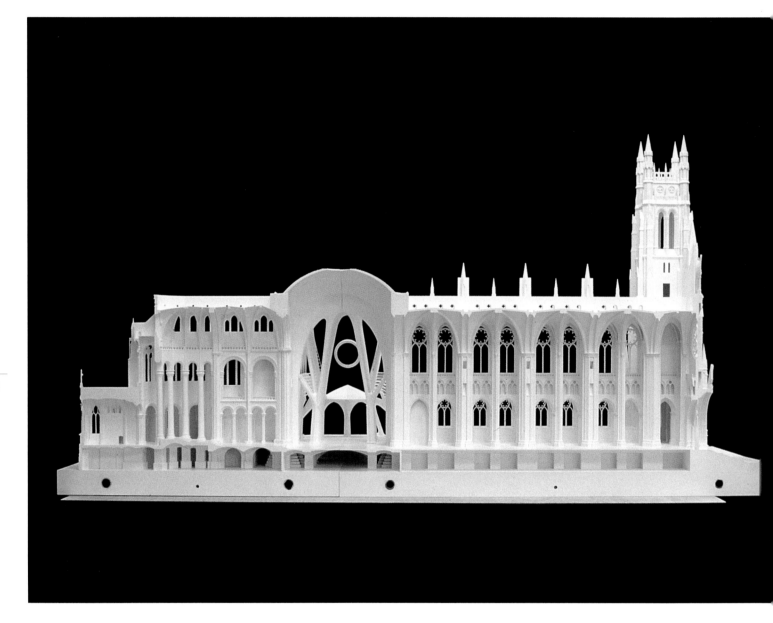

Cathedral of St. John the Divine
New York, USA
1991

Above left and right

Cathedral of St. John the Divine
New York, USA
1991

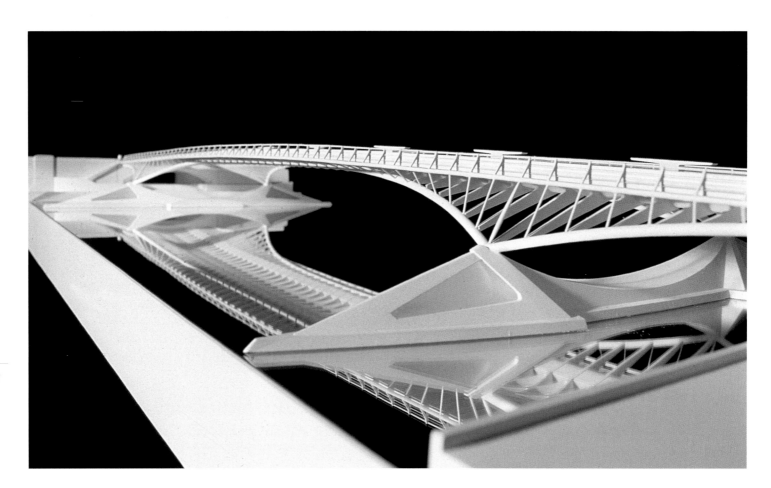

90

Solferino Footbridge
Paris, France
1992

Tenerife Exhibition Center
Tenerife, Spain
1992-95

Above and facing page

Reichstag Conversion
Berlin, Germany
1992

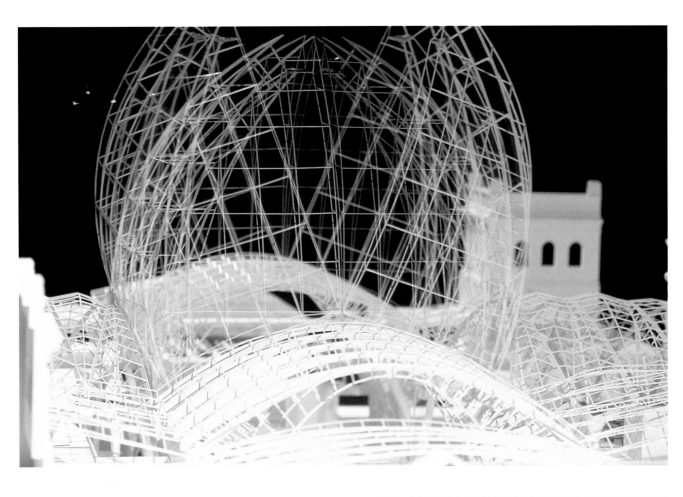

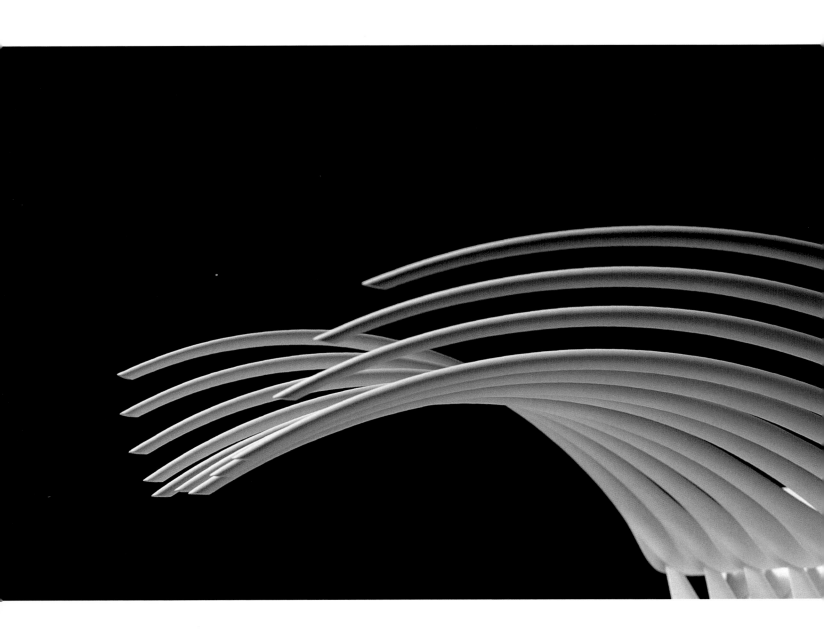

A New Paradigm

CHAPTER 3

The significance of Calatrava's current work is that it proposes not only schemes and spatial structural solutions but also a paradigm for contemporary design thinking and practice. It demonstrates that, in order to achieve a better setting for our cities and landscapes, it is not only possible but also necessary to overcome barriers among art, architecture, engineering, and philosophical reflection. Thus, his work, although grounded on technology, is unique in its capacity to generate the wildest metaphors. In its explorations of movement, we are invited to initiate dreamwork, at times in a surrealist, Buñuelesque way, at times an a Freudian way, and to experience structures breaking free from their static world, entering possible worlds where they can fulfill a wish, a desire. Beyond the satisfaction of immediate practical programmatic demands, beyond problem solving, and behind the obsession with form, there is a ludic, erotic, and enthusiastic feeling, in the original senses of these words, and also a spiritual inquiry. The work achieves a cognitive-moral provocation, the highest goal in the hierarchy of well-formed structures. The structures remind us of Spinoza's philosophy, to define a morality based on geometric reasoning, "consider(ing) human actions and desires ... manners, as though ... concerned with lines, planes, and solids." They eject didactic dogmas, reframe questions, and seduce us to inquiry, learning, and a deeper engagement.

95

Shadow Machine
New York, USA
1992-93

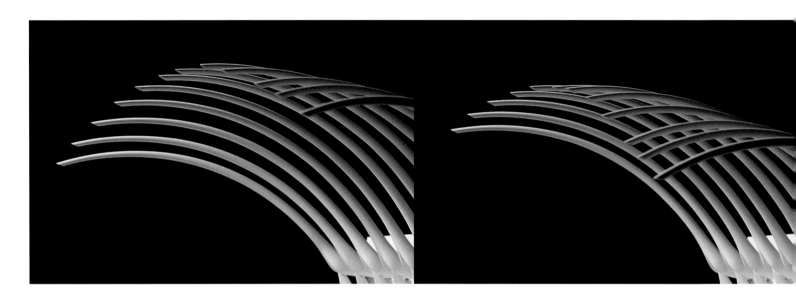

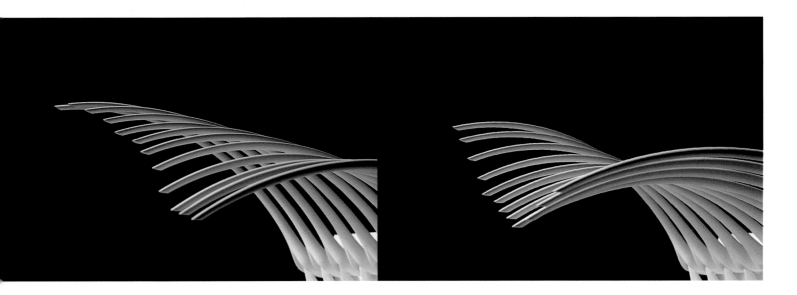

Above and facing page

Shadow Machine
New York, USA
1992-93

Alcoy Municipal Center
Alcoy, Spain
1992-95

Alcoy Municipal Center
Alcoy, Spain
1992-95

100

Alcoy Municipal Center
Alcoy, Spain
1992-95

Alcoy Municipal Center
Alcoy, Spain
1992-95

102

Alcoy Municipal Center
Alcoy, Spain
1992-95

Alcoy Municipal Center
Alcoy, Spain
1992-95

104

Alcoy Municipal Center
Alcoy, Spain
1992-95

Alcoy Municipal Center
Alcoy, Spain
1992-95

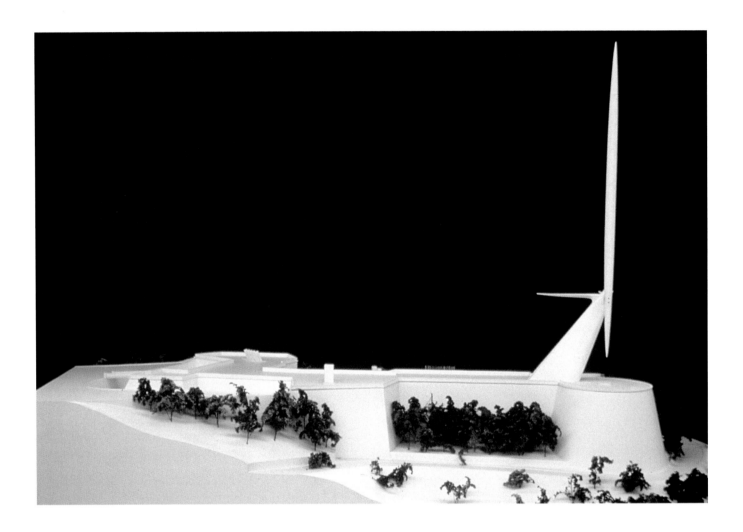

Alicante Communications Tower
Alicante, Spain
1993

Alicante Communications Tower
Alicante, Spain
1993

Oriente Station
Lisbon, Portugal
1993-98

Oriente Station
Lisbon, Portugal
1993-98

110

Oriente Station
Lisbon, Portugal
1993-98

Oriente Station
Lisbon, Portugal
1993-98

Oriente Station
Lisbon, Portugal
1993-98

Oriente Station
Lisbon, Portugal
1993-98

114

St. Paul's Footbridge
London, England
1994

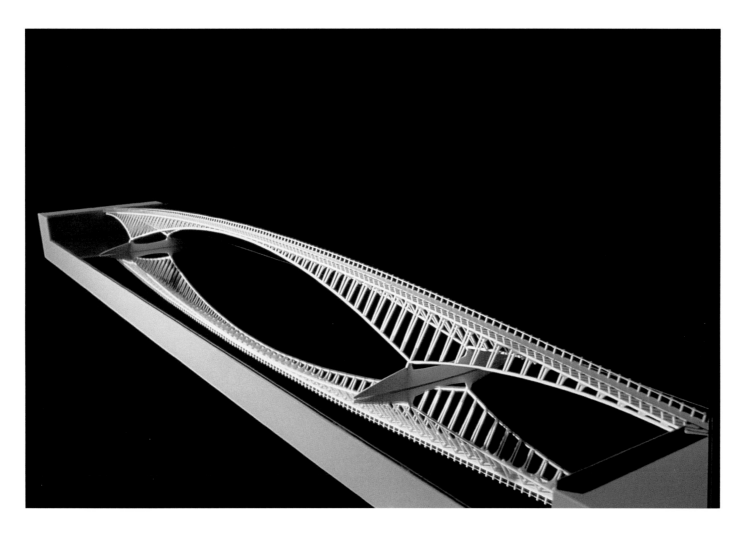

St. Paul's Footbridge

London, England

1994

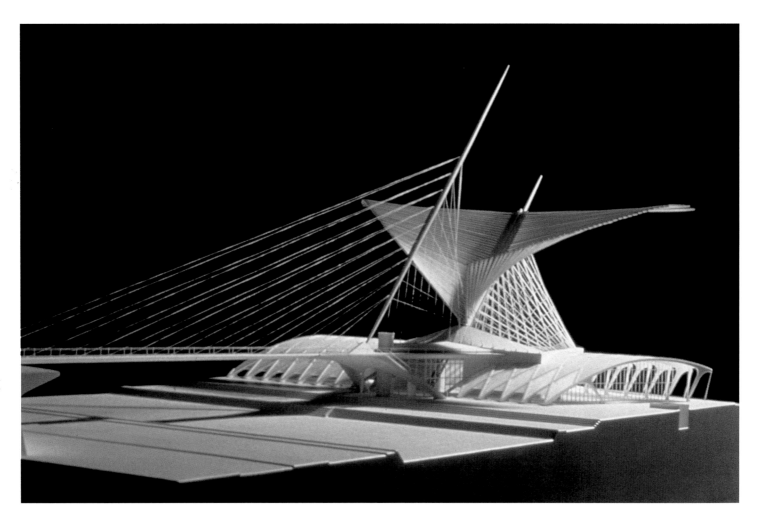

Milwaukee Art Museum
Milwaukee, USA
1994-2000

Milwaukee Art Museum
Milwaukee, USA
1994-2000

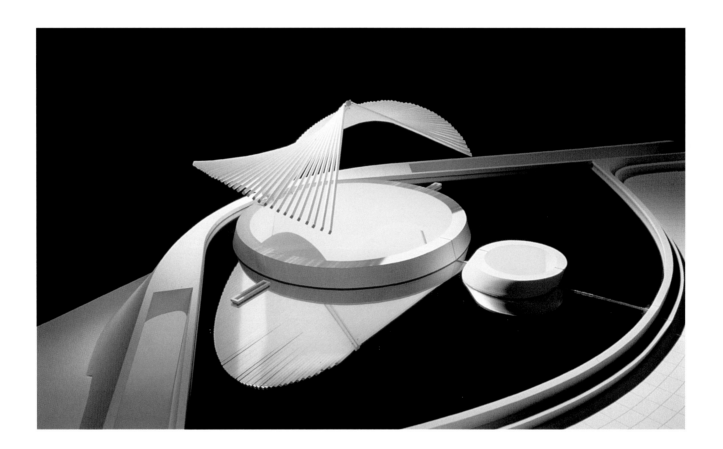

Above and facing page

Cathedral Square
Los Angeles, USA
1996

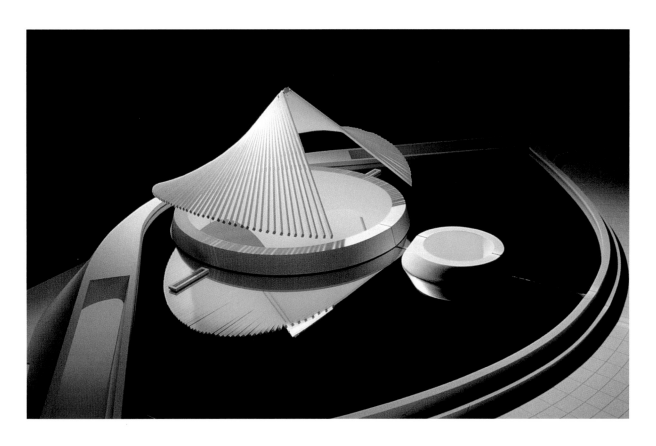

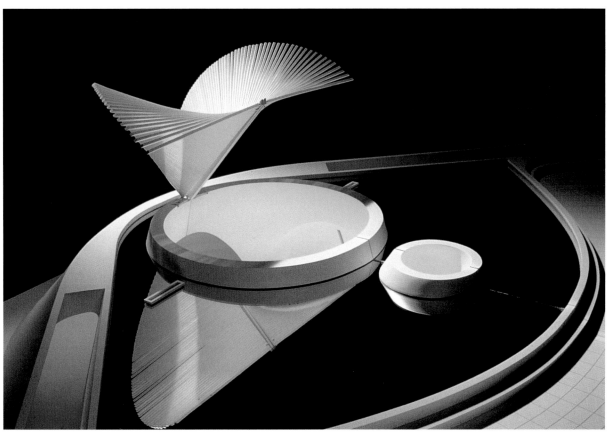

120

Orleans Bridge
Orleans, France
1996-

Orleans Bridge
Orleans, France
1996-

122

Toronto Island Airport Bridge
Toronto, Canada
1998

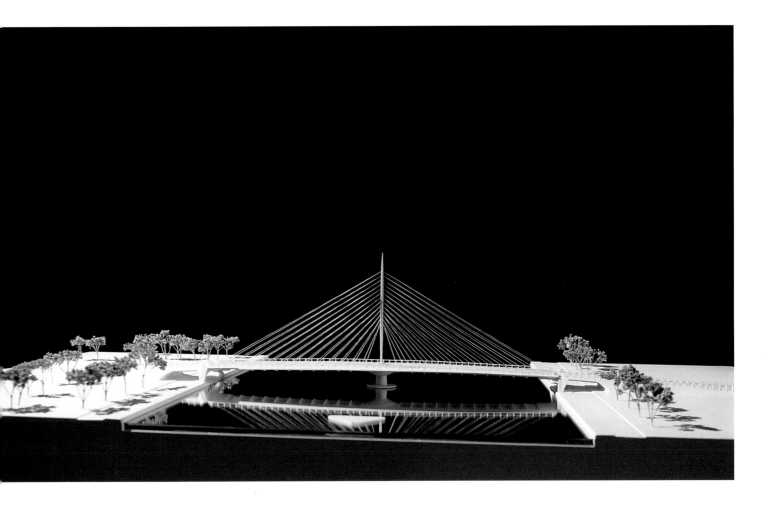

Toronto Island Airport Bridge
Toronto, Canada
1998

Sculpture
Zürich, Switzerland
1994

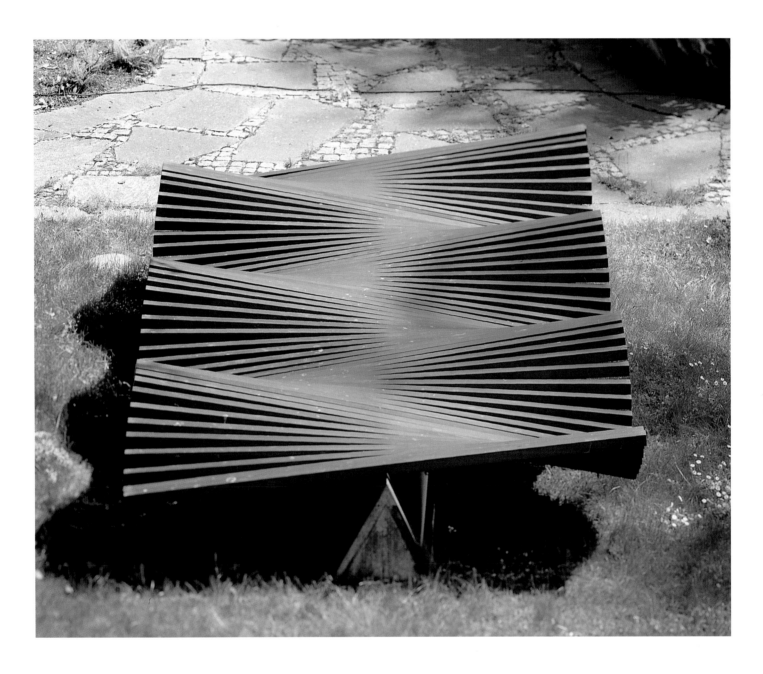

Sculpture
Zürich, Switzerland
1994

126

Sculpture
Zürich, Switzerland
1996

Sculpture
Zürich, Switzerland
1996

128

Sculpture
Zürich, Switzerland
1996

Sculpture
Zürich, Switzerland
1999

130

Sculpture
Zürich, Switzerland
1999

131

Sculpture

Zürich, Switzerland

2000

132

Sculpture
Zürich, Switzerland
2000

133

Sculpture
Zürich, Switzerland
2000

134

Two views of same sculpture study

Sculpture Study
Zürich, Switzerland
1999

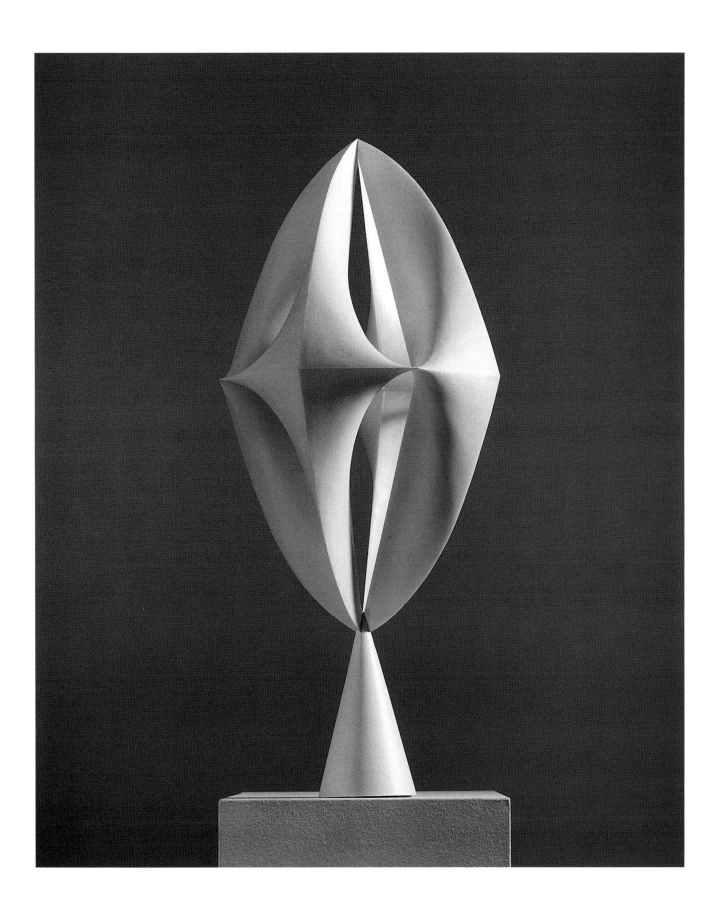

Sculpture Study
Zürich, Switzerland
1999

136

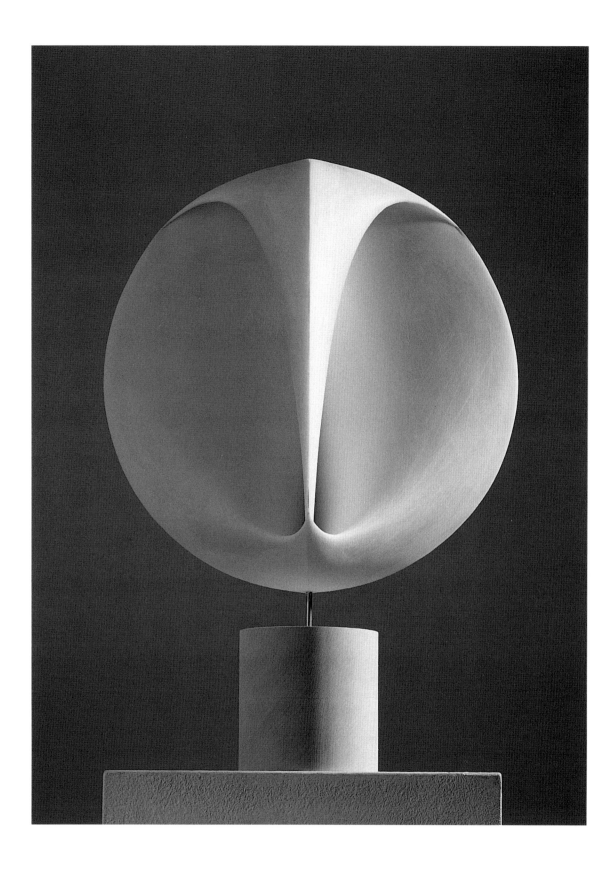

Sculpture Study
Zürich, Switzerland
1999

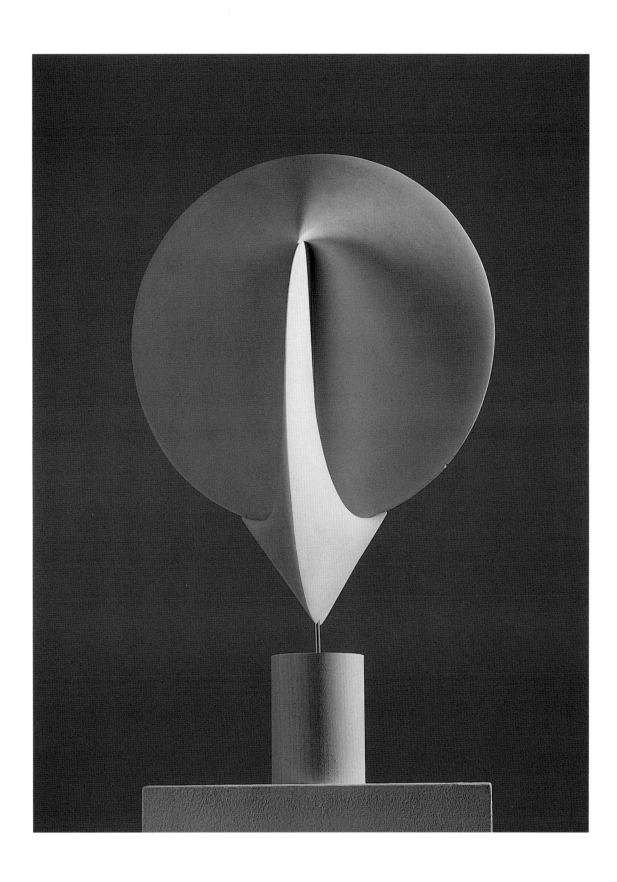

137

Sculpture Study
Zürich, Switzerland
1999

138

Sculpture Study
Zürich, Switzerland
1999

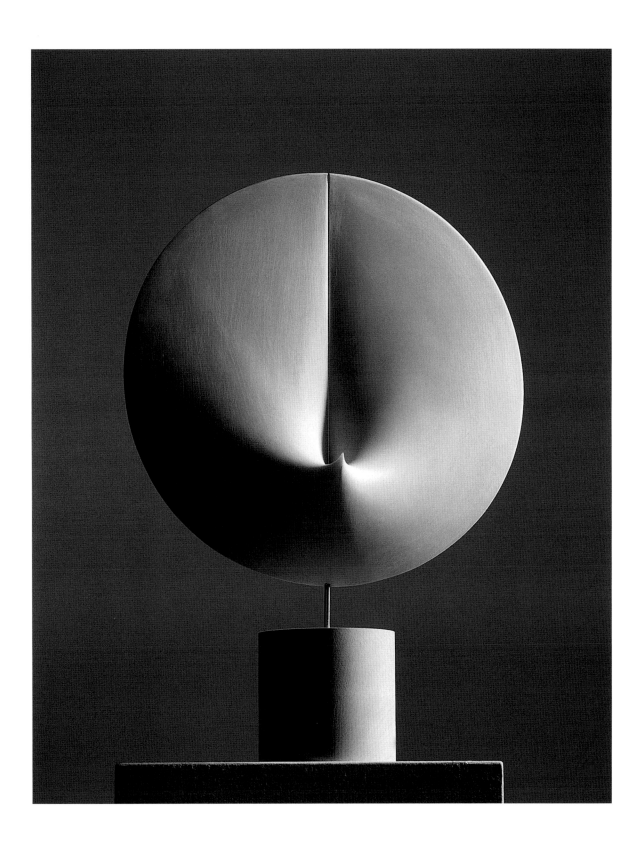

139

Sculpture Study
Zürich, Switzerland
1999

140

Sculpture Study
Zürich, Switzerland
1999

Sculpture Study
Zürich, Switzerland
1999

142

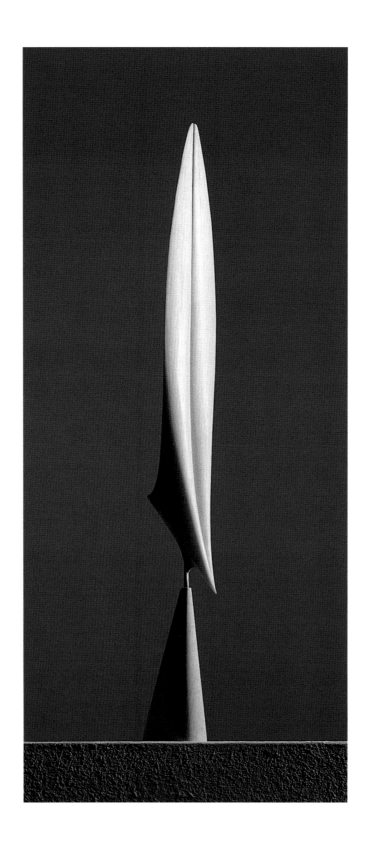

Sculpture Study
Zürich, Switzerland
1999

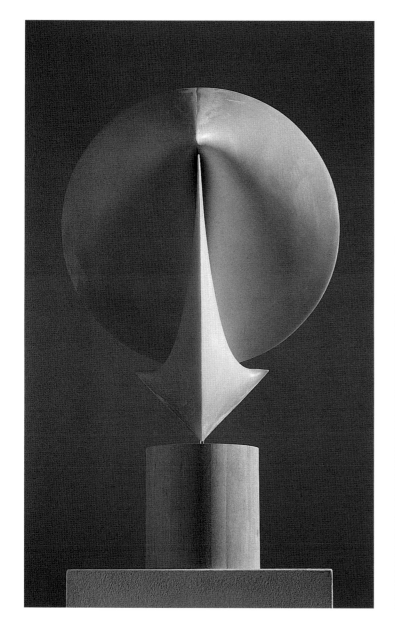

143

Two views of same sculpture study

Sculpture Study
Zürich, Switzerland
1999

144

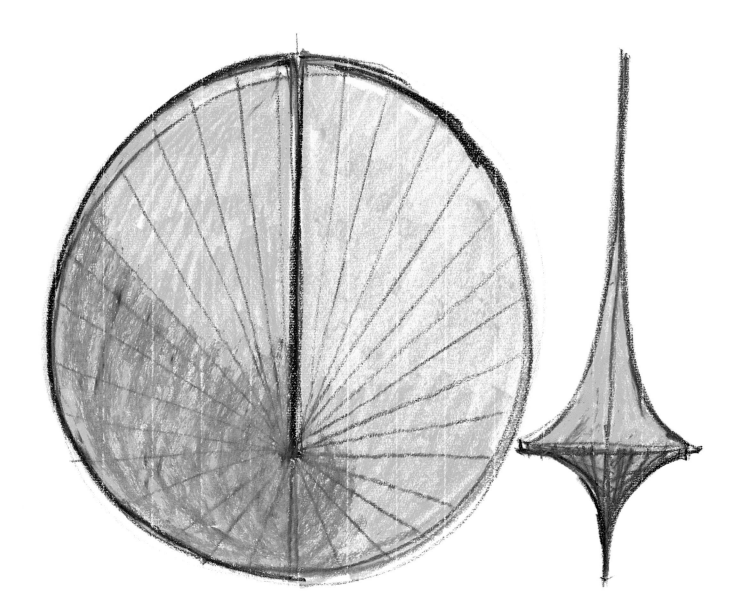

Sculpture study for facing page

Drawing
Zürich, Switzerland
1999

Sculpture
Zürich, Switzerland
1999

146

Bull
Zürich, Switzerland
1999

147

Bull
Zürich, Switzerland
1999

148

Bulls
Zürich, Switzerland
1999

Bulls
Zürich, Switzerland
1999

150

Bull
Zürich, Switzerland
1999

Bull
Zürich, Switzerland
1999

151

152

Bull
Zürich, Switzerland
1999

153

Bulls
Zürich, Switzerland
1999

154

Study for tables from bull drawings

Bulls
Zürich, Switzerland
1999

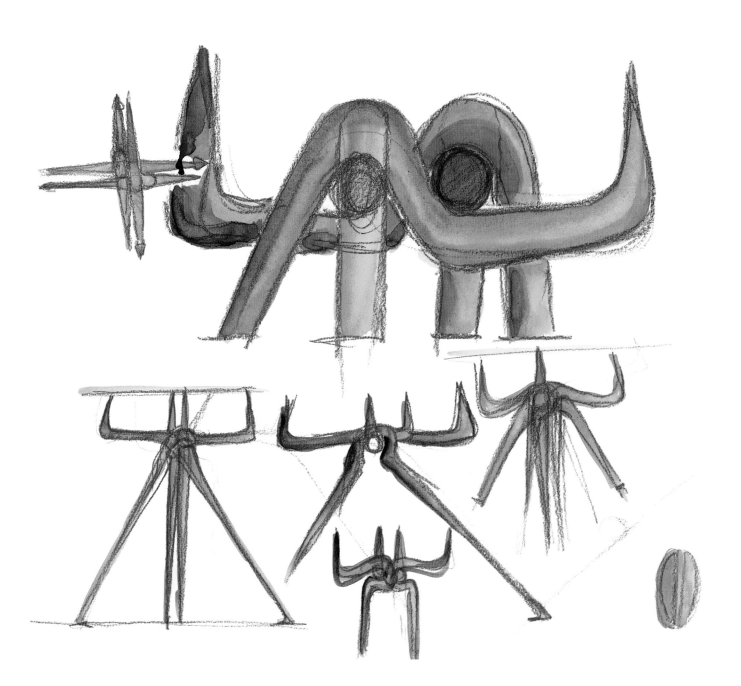

155

Study for tables from bull drawings

Bulls
Zürich, Switzerland
1999

Chronology

28 July 1951	Santiago Calatrava Valls, born in Benimamet near Valencia, Spain
1968	School graduation in Valencia
1968-1969	Attends art school in Valencia
1969-1974	Studies architecture at the Escuela Tecnica Superior de Arquitectura de Valencia, qualifying as an architect.
	Post-graduate course in Urbanism
1975-1979	Civil engineering studies at the Swiss Federal Institute of Technology (ETH), Zürich
1979-1981	Doctorate in Technical Science at the ETH, Ph.D. Dissertation, *The Foldability of Spaceframes*
	Assistant at the Institute for Building Statics and Construction and the Institute for Aerodynamics and Lightweight Construction at the ETH, Zürich
1981	Architectural and engineering practice established in Zürich
1985	*9 Sculptures by Santiago Calatrava*, exhibition at the Jamileh Weber Gallery, Zürich
1987	Member of the *BSA* (Union of Swiss Architects)
	Auguste Perret UIA Prize (Union Internationale d'Architectes), Paris

Member of the *International Academy of Architecture*

Participation at the *17th Triennale* in Milano

Santiago Calatrava, exhibition, Museum of Architecture, Basle

1988 City of Barcelona Art Prize for the *Bach de Roda-Felipe II Bridge*, Barcelona

    Premio de la Asociación de la Prensa (Press Assciation Award), Valencia

    LABSE Prize, International Association of Bridge and Structural Engineering

    FAD Prize, Fomento de las Artes y del Diseño, Spain

    Fritz Schumacher Prize for Urbanism, Architecture and Engineering, Hamburg

    Fazlur Rahman Khan International Fellowship for Architecture and Engineering

1989 Second architectural and engineering practice established in Paris

    Honorary Member of the *BDA* (Bund Deutscher Architekten)

    Santiago Calatrava, travelling exhibition, New York, St. Louis, Chicago,
Los Angeles, Toronto, Montreal

1990 *Médaille d'Argent de la Recherche et de la Technique,* Fondation Académie
d'Architecture 1970, Paris

1991 *European Glulam Award* (Glued Laminated Timber Construction), Munich

    Santiago Calatrava, exhibition, Suomen Rakennustaiteen Museum, Helsinki

    City of Zürich Award for Good Building 1991, for Stadelhofen Railway Station,
Zürich

Retrospective - Dynamic Equilibrium, exhibition, Museum of Design, Zürich

1992   CEOE Foundation, *VI Dragados y Construcciones Prize* for Alamillo Bridge

Member of the *Real Academia de Bellas Artes de San Carlos*, Valencia

Member of the *Europe Academy*, Cologne

Retrospective, exhibition, Dutch Institute for Architecture, Rotterdam

Gold Medal, Institute of Structural Engineers, London

Brunel Award, for Stadelhofen Railway Station, Zürich

Santiago Calatrava - Retrospective, exhibition, Royal Institute of British Architects, London

Retrospective, exhibition, Arkitektur Museet, Stockholm

1993   *II Honor Prize*, from the City of Pedreguer for Urban Arquitectonic Merit, Pedreguer

Santiago Calatrava - Bridges, exhibition, Deutsches Museum, Munich

Structure and Expression, exhibition, Museum of Modern Art (MoMA), New York

Hon RIBA Honorary Member of the Royal Institute of British Architects, London

Santiago Calatrava, exhibition, La Lontja Museum, Valencia

Santiago Calatrava, exhibition, Overbeck Society Pavilion, Lübeck

Santiago Calatrava, exhibition, Architecture Centre, Gammel Dok, Copenhagen

159

Doctor Honoris Causa, Polytechnic University of Valencia

Medalla de Honor al Fomento de la Invención, Fundación García Cabrerizo, Madrid

City of Toronto Urban Design Award, for the BCE Place Galeria, Toronto

World Economic Forum Davos honors Santiago Calatrava as *Global Leader for Tomorrow*

1994   *Santiago Calatrava - Recent Projects*, exhibition, Bruton Street Gallery, London

Doctor Honoris Causa, University of Seville

Santiago Calatrava - Buildings and Bridges, exhibition, Museum of Applied and Folk Arts, Moscow

Creu de Sant Jordi, Generalitat de Catalunya, Barcelona

Doctor Honoris Causa of Letters in Environmental Studies, Heriot-Watt University, Edinburgh

Santiago Calatrava - The Dynamics of Equilibrium, exhibition, Ma Gallery, Tokyo

Santiago Calatrava, exhibition, Arquería de los Nuevos Ministerios, Madrid

Santiago Calatrava, exhibition, Sala de Arte "La Recova," Santa Cruz de Tenerife

Fellow Honoris Causa, The Royal Incorporation of Architects, Scotland

Honorary Member of *Colegio de Arquitectos*, City of Mexico

1995   *Santiago Calatrava*, exhibition, Centro Cultural de Belem, Lisbon

Santiago Calatrava - Construction and Movement, exhibition, Fondazione Angelo Masieri, Venice

Doctor Honoris Causa of Science, University College, Salford

Santiago Calatrava, exhibition, Navarra Museum, Pamplona

Canton of Lucerne, *Award for Good Building 1983-1993*, for the station and square

1996   *Medalla de Oro al Mérito de las Bellas Artes*, Ministry of Culture, Granada

Santiago Calatrava, exhibition, Archivo Foral, Bilbao

Santiago Calatrava, Bewegliche Architekturen - bündel fächer welle, exhibition, Museum of Design, Zürich

Santiago Calatrava - opere e progetti 1980-1996, exhibition, Palazzo della Ragione, Padova

Mostra Internazionale di Scultura All'aperto, exhibition, Vira Gambarogno, Ascona, Bellinzona

Doctor Honoris Causa of Science, University of Strathclyde, Glasgow

Santiago Calatrava - Quatro Ponte sul Canal Grande, exhibition, Spazio Olivetti, Venice

Santiago Calatrava - Sculpture, exhibition, Government Building, St. Gallen

Santiago Calatrava - Kunst ist Bau - Bau ist Kunst, exhibition, Department of Building, Basle

Santiago Calatrava, exhibition, Milwaukee Art Museum, Milwaukee, Wisconsin

Santiago Calatrava - City Point, exhibition, Britannic Tower, London

1997   *Doctor of Science Honoris Causa*, Institute of Technology, Delft

Santiago Calatrava - Structure and Movement, exhibition, National Museum of Science, Haifa

European Award for Steel Structures, reconstruction of the "Kronprinzen-brücke," Berlin

Louis Vuiton - Moet Hennesy Art Prize, Paris

Maestro de Oro del Forum de Alta Dirección, Madrid

Doctor Honoris Causa of Engineering, Milwaukee School of Engineering, Milwaukee, Wisconsin

Structural Engineer License by the State of Illinois Department of Professional Engineering, License No. 081-005441, granted November (Renewed in 1998)

Temporary *License for the Practice of Professional Engineering* by the State of California Board of Professional Engineers and Land Surveyors (Renewed in 1998)

1998   Member of *Les Arts et Lettres*, Paris

Santiago Calatrava - Work in Progress, exhibition, *Triennale* in Milano

1988 Brunel Awards, Madrid - Station d'Oriente, Lisbon Multimodal Station S.A. Portugal

Lecture Series for the School of Architecture and Design at Massachusetts Institute of Technology, Cambridge

1999   *Doctor Honoris Causa of Civil Engineering*, Università degli studi di Cassino

Honorary Member of the *Real Academia de Bellas Artes de San Fernando*, Madrid

Principe de Asturias de las Artes prize, Spain

Doctor Honoris Causa of Technology, University of Lund

Foreign Member of the Academy, Royal Swedish Academy of Engineering
Sciences, IVA

License for the Practice of Professional Engineering by the State of Texas,
Board of Professional Engineers, License No. 85263

Grau Grande Oficial da Ordem do Mérito, Chancelaria das Ordens
Honorificas Portuguesas, Lisbon

Honorary Member of the Colegio de Ingenieros Tecnicos de Obras Publicas,
Madrid

Gold Medal, The Concrete Society, London

Honourable Mention, *Canadian Consulting Engineering Awards* for the
Mimico Creek Bridge, Toronto

2000   *Doctor Honoris Causa of Architecture*, Università degli Studi di Ferrara

        Honorary Fellowship, Royal Architectural Institute of Canada College
        of Fellows

        Algur H. Meadows Award for Excellence in the Arts, Southern Methodist
        University, Dallas

2001   *Poetics of Movement: The Architecture of Santiago Calatrava*, exhibition,
        Meadows Museum, Southern Methodist University, Dallas

163

Bibliography

Books

Blaser, W., *Santiago Calatrava: Ingenieur-Architektur, Engineering Architecture* (Basel: Birkhäuser Verlag, 1989).

Frampton, K., et al., *Calatrava Bridges* (Zürich: Artemis Verlag, 1993).

Harbison, R., *Creatures from the Mind of the Engineer: The Architecture of Santiago Calatrava* (Zürich: Artemis Verlag, 1992).

Klein, B., *Santiago Calatrava: Bahnhof Stadelhofen, Zürich* (Berlin: Wasmuth Verlag, 1993).

Sharp, D., *Santiago Calatrava* (London: Book Art / E&FN Spon, 1992).

Tischauser, A., and S. von Moos, *Calatrava Public Buildings* (Basel: Birkhäuser Verlag, 1998).

Tzonis, A., and L. Lefaivre, *Movement, Structure and the Work of Santiago Calatrava* (Basel: Birkhäuser Verlag, 1995).

Tzonis, A., *Santiago Calatrava: The Poetics of Movement* (New York: Universe Publishing, 1999).

Tzonis, A., and L. Lefaivre, *Santiago Calatrava's Creative Process. Volume I: The Dissertation, Volume II: Sketchbooks* (Basel: Birkhäuser, 2000).

Webster, A. C., and K. Frampton, *Santiago Calatrava: Schule und Museum für Gestaltung* (Zürich: Schriftenreihe 15, 1992).

Zardini, M., and F. Motta, *Santiago Calatrava* (Milan: Libro Segreto, 1995).

Catalogues, Special Issues, Project Monographs

Calatrava, S., *Dynamische Gleichgewichte: neue Projekte* (Zürich: Artemis Verlag, 1991).

Cullen, M.S., and M. Kieren, *Calatrava: Berlin Five Projects* (Basel: Birkhäuser Verlag, 1994).

Hauser, H., *Kontroverse Beitrage zu einem unstrittenen Bautypus* (Stuttgart: 1993).

Klein, B., et al., *Ein Bahnof / Une Gare* (Heiden: Archithese, 1990).

Le Roux, M., and M. Rivoire, *Calatrava* (Grenoble: Escale Satolas, 1994).

McQuaid, M., *Santiago Calatrava: Structure and Expression* (New York: Museum of Modern Art, 1993).

Molinari, L., *Santiago Calatrava* (Milan: Skira, 1998).

Nicolin, P., "Santiago Calatrava, il folle volo" (*Quaderni di Lotus 7,* Milan: Electa, 1987).

Polano, S., *Santiago Calatrava,* Documenti di Architettura (Milan: Electa, 1996).

Santiago Calatrava (Valencia: Generalitat Valenciana, 1986).

Santiago Calatrava (Zürich: Galerie Jamileh Weber, 1986).

"Santiago Calatrava 1983-93" (Valencia: 1993; reprinted as an editorial in *El Croquis,* Madrid, 1993).

Santiago Calatrava: El Croquis, vol. 38 (Madrid: 1989).

Santiago Calatrava: El Croquis, vol. 47 (Madrid: 1992).

Santiago Calatrava, 1983-1996 (Madrid: AV-Monografias, 1996).

Santiago Calatrava: The Dynamics of Equilibrium (Tokyo: Ma Gallery, 1994).

This publication was produced on the occasion of the exhibition,
Poetics of Movement: The Architecture of Santiago Calatrava ,
and the opening of the new Meadows Museum
on the campus of Southern Methodist University, Dallas.

Mr. Calatrava is the 15th recipient of the
Algur H. Meadows Awards for
Excellence in the Arts.

The exhibition was held March 25-August 5, 2001.

Following page

Calatrava's human figures, watercolor